BREAD CRUMBS

VOLUME 1

Inspirational Thoughts and Motivational Quotes

Dr. FAY MAUREEN

M⊙tivational PRESS®
LEADERS IN GLOBAL PUBLISHING

Published by Motivational Press, Inc.
7777 N Wickham Rd, # 12-247
Melbourne, FL 32940
www.MotivationalPress.com

Copyright 2014 © by Fay Maureen Butler

All Rights Reserved

No part of this book may be reproduced or transmitted in any form by any means: graphic, electronic, or mechanical, including photocopying, recording, taping or by any information storage or retrieval system without permission, in writing, from the authors, except for the inclusion of brief quotations in a review, article, book, or academic paper. The authors and publisher of this book and the associated materials have used their best efforts in preparing this material. The authors and publisher make no representations or warranties with respect to accuracy, applicability, fitness or completeness of the contents of this material. They disclaim any warranties expressed or implied, merchantability, or fitness for any particular purpose. The authors and publisher shall in no event be held liable for any loss or other damages, including but not limited to special, incidental, consequential, or other damages. If you have any questions or concerns, the advice of a competent professional should be sought.

Manufactured in the United States of America.

ISBN: 978-1-62865-079-2

Yes Lord I'll Take The Crumbs

If I gather enough crumbs, I will have a slice of bread.

If I gather enough slices, I will have a Loaf.

Yes Lord, I will take the Crumbs

THE BREAD OF LIFE

Eat the crumbs, make your loaf and live

CONTENTS

—∞⃟⃟∞—

ACKNOWLEDGEMENTS

To God be the Glory. I thank God for life and I want to please him in everything I do for the balance of my days......In Him I live, Move and Have my being

To The memory of My Father - Pastor/ Attorney John L. Butler- A Giant of a Dad and a Great Man of God.

To my Family

Mother - Dr. Fay Ellis Butler... The Mother..... so many of my talents... I Inherited from her

Siblings - Glenda, James, Terrence, Jacqueline, Eric, Cynthia, Esther, Tyrone, Racquel

Aunts - Dolores, Beatrice, Joy, Bernice, Sylvia, Janey, Ethel, Eleanor

Uncles: Frederick, David, Nicky, A. Baker

My Many Cousins

WOMEN OF GOD

Mothers - L Van Zandt, G Washington, F Tompkins

Sister friends - Denise K, Tracee W, Brenda W, Cordelia W, Linda J, Joyce R, Patti B, Sonya E, Nejla H, Regina M

COVENANT BROTHERS

Pastor Roland, Pastor Kevin, Pastor Rogers

BUSINESS AFFILIATES

Steve A, Cedric W

CHURCHES

Salvation and Restoration Christian Church of God In Christ

Upper Room International Ministries COGIC-where I serve as Pastor

FRIENDS OF UPPER ROOM AND HULDAHS HOSUE

Ministry Couples who pray for me- The Thomas Family (NC) The LaRose Family (NY) The Brocketts (NY)

Prophets - Kothapally (India) Isuzu (Kenya) Evans (NC) Vickers (NY) Johnson(NY) Holcomb(NY)

Lethia West Wooten who spoke the word and sparked the idea for Breadcrumbs

Michelle Hermonstyne Headley.....

Lucille Houston- Model of Faithfulness

FOREWORD

This is not the average assignment. These are the words that were spoken to Dr Fay as she accepted the responsibility to be the Pastor of a small congregation in Brooklyn, NY.

Having faced breast cancer and career challenges, Dr Fay embraced these words with a passion and fearlessness to serve the underserved and those in need.

It is Dr. Fays courage and perseverance that has helped her to succeed against many odds. Often questioning why, when and how, she never left her post when she faced discouragement and despair. Looking back she now realizes that, in her words "it was a little church in Brooklyn" that opened the door to the "unlimited potential that was waiting to be stirred up". She learned that success wasn't in numbers or a big crowd, but in the timely use of maximizing available resources.

Today many of her dreams and visions have become reality. Dr Fay hosts a nationally syndicated web radio show, She also hosts a WebTV show that is seen in the United States and abroad, the "drfaymaureen" brand across multiple social networking sites is known for excellence and inspiration. She has started a social media strategy firm, all while working in higher education.

I have had the privilege of working with, researching, and writing on a number of visionaries and great writers. A common thread among them is that they never quit and always found the inner strength to continue in the face of challenging circumstances.

As you take the daily journey through this first volume of Bread-crumbs...be inspired by the person who has experienced this journey. Dr Fay is not like the others and this is not the average motivational book.

To Your Success,

Justin Sachs

International Best Selling Author of The Power of Persistence

Yes Lord I Will Take the Crumbs..........

Matthew 15 (NIV)

²⁵ The woman came and knelt before him. "Lord, help me!" she said.

²⁶ He replied, "It is not right to take the children's bread and toss it to the dogs."

²⁷ "Yes it is, Lord," she said. "Even the dogs eat the crumbs that fall from their master's table."

²⁸ Then Jesus said to her, "Woman, you have great faith! Your request is granted." And her daughter was healed at that moment.

Mark 7 (KJV)

²⁵ For a certain woman, whose young daughter had an unclean spirit, heard of him, and came and fell at his feet:

²⁶ The woman was a Greek, a Syrophenician by nation; and she besought him that he would cast forth the devil out of her daughter.

²⁷ But Jesus said unto her, Let the children first be filled: for it is not meet to take the children's bread, and to cast it unto the dogs.

²⁸ And she answered and said unto him, Yes, Lord: yet the dogs under the table eat of the children's crumbs.

²⁹ And he said unto her, For this saying go thy way; the devil is gone out of thy daughter.

³⁰ And when she was come to her house, she found the devil gone out, and her daughter laid upon the bed.

Introduction.... Crumbs...

Yes Lord, I will take the Crumbs.

Lord I will work with the crumbs if they come from you. I may have been looking for a whole loaf, but I will take the crumbs.

If you give me enough crumbs from the masters table, I will collect the crumbs until I get enough for a slice, then a loaf.

The crumbs you give me are better than the choicest of foods anywhere else.

He said to the woman - Great is your faith.

Her daughter was healed, she received a miracle.

Day One

Breadcrumbs for life

Don't be so indifferent to dysfunction that you accept it as the new normal.

Breadcrumbs for work

In your absence, let your presence be felt, Finish "dated" business before you leave for a break.

Day Two

Breadcrumbs for life

The Detour was the divine pathway to
multiplicity of blessings...

Inspirational Thought

Seasons of Multiplicity-Apply to Ministry
and Marketplace:
Cast Your Nets Far and Wide.
Shoot Your Arrows Repeatedly.
Cast Your Bread upon Many Waters.

Day Three

Breadcrumbs for life

The story behind the completed vision
builds endurance, increases faith and
expands your knowledge.
There is always a story behind the
completed vision. Admire the outcome, but
Respect the Journey.

Breadcrumbs for work

You DON'T need "POSITION" POWER to
be a person of INFLUENCE.

Day Four

Breadcrumbs for life

Seeing the moment allows you to seize the moment - Timing is everything! Understand the opportune moment and make the most of it or act appropriately.

Breadcrumbsforwork

Stewardship of Opportunity is Critical- Maximize the Moment.

Inspirational Thought

STEWARDSHIP OF OPPORTUNITY IS
CRITICAL!... Be very careful, then, how you
live—not as unwise but as wise, MAKING
THE MOST OF EVERY OPPORTUNITY,
because the days are evil. Therefore do not
be foolish, but understand what the Lord's
will is.

(Ephesians 5:15-17 NIV)

(Timing is everything! Discerning is
understanding the opportune moment and
to redeem is to make the most of it or act
appropriately, thus you enter the Season of
Manifestation of particular things.)

Day Five

Breadcrumbs for life

STUDY TO BE QUIET! Don't be a
"CARRIER" of Confusion, Division and
Chaos, DON'T accept, believe,repeat every
RUMOR you hear.

Breadcrumbsforwork

Everything you do today influences your
tomorrow, be careful with your words,
where you go and how you treat others.

Day Six

Breadcrumbs for life

Don't DESPISE SMALL beginnings, start
somewhere, use what is in your hands, stay
humble, be a lifelong learner.

Inspirational Thought

THE ANSWER IS RIGHT IN FRONT OF YOU, THE SEED IS IN YOUR HAND, BE STILL, If you don't see the ANSWER, ASK GOD TO TAKE THE SCALES OFF OF YOUR NATURAL AND SPIRITUAL EYES. (Exodus 4:2) and the Lord said to him (Moses) what is that in your hand? And he said a Rod...USE THE ROD IN YOUR HANDS! What Rod: praying, singing, baking, sewing, poetry writing, preaching, teaching, giving, driving the church van, painting, drawing, writing, website building, audiovisual excellence, financial acumen.......DO YOU GET THE PICTURE...THE ANSWER IS RIGHT IN FRONT OF YOU IN YOUR HAND!

Be A Good Steward of What is In Your Hand. Use it for the Kingdom and stand back and Watch God.

Day Seven

Breadcrumbs for life

Let Gods Agenda Supersede your agenda.

Breadcrumbs for work

Dedication, diligence and the desire to succeed overcome defeat and disappointment.

Day Eight

Breadcrumbs for life

There are always "PreSeasons" before the real....."New" Seasons.....Discern the seasons, adjust your behavior.......

Breadcrumbsforwork

Workplace advancement-use the time during career detours to become a subject matter expert in another area-redo you.

Day Nine

Breadcrumbs for life

Handle With Care Your Godly Assignments.

Breadcrumbs for work

Be skillful in assessing the talents of those you supervise and then Manage your talent.

Day Ten

Breadcrumbs for work

Project Management-Visualization-"See The End" at the beginning. Create a list FROM your "END PICTURE."

Inspirational Thought

Formative and Summative Assessment for Ministry Initiatives. Formative assessment you tweak and modify as needed during the course of the project: Summative assessment, once the project is complete, you review what worked and what did not work and make necessary adjustments.
In my opinion, with the help of the Holy Ghost, our initiatives will be most effective if we practice FORMATIVE AND SUMMATIVE ASSESSMENT and as you seek God, pray in the spirit, remain submissive and obedient, the innovative ideas and strategies will be plentiful.
Another way to explain-formative assessment-As you cook-you taste and test the dish and make changes-summative assessment is when you serve it to others and they taste and test and give feedback on what changes if any need to be made.

Day Eleven

Breadcrumbs for life

Dream Killers, Negative Destiny Alterers,
Direction Changers... Separate From.

Breadcrumbsforwork

Write the Vision of where you want to
go…..Stay on the path of your vision.

Inspirational Thought

THE THREE D's Can lead to LIFE OR
DEATH: Dreams, Destiny and Direction:
STAY in the Secret Place of the Most High,
STAY focused and Keep your eyes on the
Prize(s), Reward (s) God has for you.

Day Twelve

Breadcrumbs for life

Complete God's assignments within HIS
"SET" time frame. Discern the time within
the season.

Breadcrumbs for work

Don't get left behind-understand the "work
ethic" culture of your environment and
model behavior.

Day Thirteen

Breadcrumbs for life

Hide in Plain Sight-and Stay ready... you
are up next.

Breadcrumbs for work

Understand Diversity in the workplace, the
person who holds the key to the next level,
or promotion, may not look like you, talk
like you or believe like you do.

Day Fourteen

Breadcrumbs for life

Keep your appointments during seasons of disappointment… it will lead to the appointed time.

Inspirational Thought

Understand what type of behavior and the corresponding required actions needed during seed time and during harvest time. It is possible to experience both seasons- seed time and harvest- in various areas of life/ ministry simultaneously.

Day Fifteen

Breadcrumbs for life

Plan For Your Expectations.

Breadcrumbs for work

Expand your "experience portfolio" volunteer for short term assignments outside of your normal duties.

Day Sixteen

Breadcrumbs for life

The Blessings, the miracles..They are looking for you NOW-Stay hidden in God-They will find you.

Breadcrumbs for work

Keep a positive outlook when interacting with difficult persons, your positive disposition yields many benefits.

Day Seventeen

Breadcrumbs for life

Don't Miss the PROMISE because of
DISOBEDIENCE....

Breadcrumbs for work

Your visual presentation and daily
conversation will either help or hurt you,
choose your words and wardrobe carefully.

Day Eighteen

Breadcrumbs for life

Delay, Denial and Disappointment
sometimes prerequisites to Acceleration,
Approval and Appointment.

Inspirational Thought

MANY ARE CALLED BUT FEW ARE CHOSEN. From Calling to Commissioning is a Process, a Journey that God Designs. Let God Commission you, not Man. Sometimes we see successful persons but we dont understand their Journey: Hidden hours of prayer, fasting, tears, oft misunderstood, humiliation, Disappointment, failure, failure again, rejection, loneliness. Let God Order your Steps. THERE is a beginning, a middle and an end to every Journey. Delay, Denial and disappointment are part of the maturation process, don't leave THE PROCESS UNTIL GOD IS FINISHED. WAIT ON GOD!

Day Nineteen

Breadcrumbs for life

ASK HIM, HE WILL SHOW/SHEW YOU! In all thy ways acknowledge him, and he shall direct thy paths. (Proverbs 3:6 KJV)

Breadcrumbs for work

Be in the Know- Obtain a "seat" at the meeting "before" the main meeting or the meeting "after" the main meeting. Why? These meetings are usually where agenda's are planned and decisions are made.

Day Twenty

Breadcrumbs for life

Die to SELF TONIGHT So you can Live
for Christ Tomorrow .... TOMORROW has
Come TODAY.

Breadcrumbs for work

Love God More Than Anything or Anyone.

Day Twenty One

Breadcrumbs for life

Your faith needs your feet to start walking-
Pastor Roland Pollard.

Breadcrumbs for work

Successfully completing challenging
assignments is a confidence builder.

Day Twenty Two

Breadcrumbs for life

Years of toiling, days of faithfulness, hidden hours of fasting and praying, Years, Days,Hours…
SUDDENLY OPEN REWARDS.

Inspirational Thought

ARE YOU A PARTICIPANT IN HEAVEN'S OPEN REWARDS PROGRAM? But thou when thou prayest, enter into thy closet, and when thou hast shut thy door, pray to thy Father which is in secret; and thy Father which seeth in secret shall REWARD THEE OPENLY..That thou appear not unto men to fast, but unto thy Father which is in secret: and thy Father, which seeth in secret, shall REWARD THEE OPENLY. (Matthew 6:6,18)

Day Twenty Three

Breadcrumbs for life

God DOWNLOADS to us what we need to UPLOAD to"our" world + "THE" WORLD. Keep space available for his continuous downloads.

Breadcrumbs for work

Don't allow your worldview to negatively impact someone else's creativity, Remain flexible.

Day Twenty Four

Breadcrumbs for life

Boaz Noticed Ruth as she gleaned during the Harvest.

Breadcrumbs for work

Get Noticed for your ability to mediate and negotiate instead of your ability to instigate or irritate.

Day Twenty Five

Breadcrumbs for life

Nevertheless at thy word I will let down the net. Let the word do the work. (Luke 5:5)

Inspirational Thoughts

THE POWER OF THE WORD (S)
LET THE WORD DO THE WORK! He sent his word, and healed them, and delivered them from their destructions. (Psalms 107:20 KJV)
He sendeth forth his commandment upon earth: his word runneth very swiftly. He sendeth out his word, and melteth them: he causeth his wind to blow, and the waters flow. He sheweth his word unto Jacob, his statutes and his judgments unto Israel. (Psalms 147:15, 18, 19 KJV)

HE HAS COME FOR YOUR WORDS..IT IS "DAY 22", For 21 DAYS, FOR SOME, "21 YEARS", THE ENEMY HAS CAUSED DELAYS...BUT ANGELS WITH FLAMING SWORDS HAVE BATTLED FOR YOU in the heavenlies..while you kept PRAYING AND FASTING! DAY 22..HE HAS COME FOR YOUR WORDS...And he said unto me, O Daniel, a man greatly beloved, understand the words that I speak unto thee, and stand upright: for unto thee am I now sent. And when he had spoken this word unto me, I stood trembling. Then said he unto me, Fear not, Daniel: for from the first day that thou didst set thine heart to understand, and to chasten thyself before thy God, thy words were heard, and I am come for thy words. But the prince of the kingdom of Persia withstood me one and twenty days: but, lo, Michael, one of the chief princes, came to help me; and I remained there with the kings of Persia.

(Daniel 10:11-13 KJV)

Day Twenty Six

Breadcrumbs for life

God First In Everything adds all things to
your any.....thing.

Breadcrumbsforwork

A Good Brand equals Market Sustainability.

Day Twenty Seven

Breadcrumbs for life

Sow "IN" season, Reap "DUE" season.

Breadcrumbs for work

INNOVATION AND CREATIVITY IS having the ability or skill to take ONE thing and develop it into MANY THINGS.

Inspirational Thought

Some of you will demonstrate a substantial RETURN on what God Invested in you in years past....some seeds when planted need many seasons before the crop can be harvested.

Day Twenty Eight

Breadcrumbs for life

STAND AND WITHSTAND! when you STAND on the Word of God, you can WITHSTAND attacks from the enemy and your enemies.

Inspirational Thought

GOD HAS NOT FORGOT! And God
REMEMBERED Noah, and every living thing,
(Genesis 8:1aKJV)

And the Lord VISITED Sarah as he had said, and
the Lord did unto Sarah as he had spoken.
(Genesis 21:1 KJV)

And he said unto Jesus, Lord, REMEMBER me
when thou comest into thy kingdom. And Jesus
said unto him, Verily I say unto thee, To day shalt
thou be with me in paradise.
(Luke 23:42, 43 KJV)

For God is not unrighteous TO FORGET your
work and labour of love, which ye have shewed
toward his name, in that ye have ministered to
the saints, and do minister.
(Hebrews 6:10 KJV)

Day Twenty Nine

Breadcrumbs for life

Reaching Gods …destination(s) in your life
yields manifestation of the promises ON
HIS TERMS!.....And this is the confidence
that we have in him, that, if we ask any thing
ACCORDING TO HIS WILL, he heareth us:
And if we know that he hear us, whatsoever
we ask, we know that we have the petitions
that we desired of him.

(1 John 5:14, 15 KJV)

Day Thirty

Breadcrumbs for life

Great Things are in small blessings.
-Michelle Headley

Breadcrumbs for work

Hardships Happen, Pick Up the Pieces,
Power Up the Remains....Move on.

Day Thirty One

Breadcrumbs for life

Build your Tabernacle for God and meet him there Consistently.

Breadcrumbsforwork

Take the good and bad moments. Make the best of it.

MOTIVATIONAL MOMENTS

Walk In Authority

WE ARE NOT IGNORANT OF SATAN'S
devices, traps, tricks, snares or schemes.
ALTHOUGH HE HAS "CHANGED" THE
"LOCK" You HAVE THE SET OF KEYS To
unlock THE DOORS of your purposes, plans,
and "exceedingly above blessings" USE YOUR
KEYS and in some cases.... Add a dose of fasting
with your prayer.

From the Desk of Dr. Fay
Steps to Success

Produce More than You Consume
A Motivational thought and prayer for
Entrepreneurs
On this year let us not just consume goods, but
let US PRODUCE GOODS AND SERVICES
for others to consume....I pray that God will
download ideas/ witty inventions and stir up
abilities and talents, and that he will give us
determination, tenacity and desire to succeed,
In Jesus name.... (Thanks for the thought...
Lakweshia Tibbs Ewing.)

Formulas for Success

Promotion
Studying for the test+taking the test+passing
the test=Promotion.

Increase
Launch out into DEEP WATERS+Spiritual
Tenacity+Trust in God+Fasting and Prayer=
Miracles and Expansion.

THE BEST FROM DR FAY'S BLOGS ON WORDPRESS

Favor

Thought...HEAR+WATCH+WAIT=LIFE and FAVOUR...Blessed is the man that heareth me, watching daily at my gates, waiting at the posts of my doors. For whoso findeth me findeth life, and shall obtain favour of the Lord. (Proverbs 8:34, 35 KJV)

GOD GRANTS FAVOUR FOR HIS PURPOSE. And Esther obtained FAVOUR in the sight of ALL THEM that looked upon her. (Esther 2:15) And the King held out to Esther the golden sceptre that was in his hand. (Esther 5:2) Then the king held out the golden sceptre toward Esther. (Esther 8:4) GOD's FAVOUR saved a nation... God Shifts circumstances, (Vashti removed) creates a process for us to COMPLETE (Esther's preparation), FAVOUR GRANTED... God then presents our ASSIGNMENT WITH HIS FAVOUR (Esther Saved a Nation).

RISE UP AND BUILD

"Rise up and Build"...... GOD has raised a "Cyrus" for your circumstance! THE ASSIGNMENT will be completed. Thus saith the Lord to his anointed, to Cyrus, whose right hand I have holden, to subdue nations before him; and I will loose the loins of kings, to open before him the two leaved gates; and the gates shall not be shut; (Isaiah 45:1 KJV)Thus saith Cyrus king of Persia, The Lord God of heaven hath given me all the kingdoms of the earth; and he hath charged me to build him an house at Jerusalem, which is in Judah. (Ezra 1:2 KJV) Then I told them of the hand of my God which was good upon me; as also the king's words that he had spoken unto me. And they said, Let us rise up and build. So they strengthened their hands for this good work. (Nehemiah 2:18 KJV)

THE GIFT OF TIME

What time is it? How much time to I have? What time is the meeting? What time is your flight? What time will you be home? .... When we think of time, we normally associate time with our daily routine. Time moves us from minute to minute, hour to hour, day to day, year to year. Time is progressive and constantly moving.

It's a God moment, have you ever thought or said that about something that has happened in your life that you knew it was "right place/right time". Those kind of opportune moments don't just happen. God orchestrates time and seasons for us to fulfill his purpose. Even when we don't always do what we need to do, God has a plan and his ways are higher than our ways and our thoughts, he orchestrates moments for his benefit.

God created Time for man to use to accomplish life's tasks but also to fulfill his purpose. It is his gift to us and we must use it properly. We cannot mishandle the gift of "Time". Time is a God thing. We may never completely understand it as God sees it, but it is our responsibility to handle what he has given to us. I am going to look at this Gift of Time from two ways: Time and Our Daily Walk (Chronos) and (Kairos)-Gods Opportune time. I hope that as you read this, you will be provoked to think of managing God's gift of time in the most strategic manner possible.

The ancient Greeks had two words for time, chronos and kairos. While the former refers to   chronological or sequential time, the latter signifies a time in between, a moment of indeterminate time in which something special happens. Kairos (καιρός) is an ancient Greek word meaning the right or opportune moment (the supreme moment).What the special something is depends on who is using the word. While chronos is quantitative, kairos has a qualitative nature.[1](Wikipedia) Chronos is the routine time, how we manage the clock, the designations of the clock. Kairos is strategic or opportune time. While these terms are spate and have distinct meanings, I believe when we manage the Chronos according to Gods plan, it turns in to the Kairos.

1st Chronicles 12:32- SONS OF ISSACHAR knew the times and knew what ISRAEL SHOULD DO. PRAY, ASK GOD TO HELP YOU WALK IN THE "Issachar" anointing to accurately discern not just your times and seasons but what your church or ministry should plan for in the future. SEIZE THE MOMENT, YOU CANT SEIZE THE MOMENT IF YOU MISS IT. THE ISSACHAR ANOINTING UNDERSTANDS TIME AND HAS A SPECIAL ABILITY TO CREATE AND PLAN THINGS AT THE RIGHT TIME...TIMING.

Hiding In Plain Sight!

God will Hide us from our enemy(ies) while we are in their midst. The witness protection program in the United States allows persons to completely change their identities so that they are hidden from "enemies". God's Witness Protection Program HIDES his witnesses (the saints) during certain seasons while he, the Almighty God, deals with the enemy. During this time God only requires that we STAND BACK and allow him to keep us hidden until he is ready for us to be revealed where he GETS ALL of the GLORY AND HONOR. People can watch you, observe you and even see many of the things God is doing for you BUT IN TIME God WILL REVEAL, GOD WILL BLESS, GOD WILL…. You will be standing and sitting in the middle of your enemies but they CANT TOUCH YOU Because GOD has hidden you!!! Psalm 32:7 You are a hiding place for me; you preserve me from trouble; you surround me with shouts of deliverance. Selah Psalm 119:114:You are my hiding place and my shield; I hope in your word.Psalm 17:8:Keep me as the apple of your eye; hide me in the shadow of your wings,Psalm 27:5:For he will hide me in his shelter in the day of trouble; he will conceal me under the cover of his tent; he will lift me high upon a rock.

Psalm 31:20:In the cover of your presence you hide them from the plots of men; you store them in your shelter from the strife of tongues. Psalm 64:2:Hide me from the secret plots of the wicked, from the throng of evildoers,Isaiah 32:2:Each will be like a hiding place from the wind, a shelter from the storm, like streams of water in a dry place, like the shade of a great rock in a weary land. PRAY THIS PRAYER, Father in the Name of Jesus, Hide Me from the enemy, help me to dwell in the SECRET PLACE as you deal with the enemy and at the appointed time, you will reveal your GLORY, MAJESTY AND POWER, in Jesus Name amen.....

GOT GAME - "SEE THE BALL , SEE THE MAN"

A Basketball sports Analogy..ON DEFENSE…SEE THE BALL, SEE THE MAN, YELLS THE BASKETBALL COACH! What he/she means is that you concentrate on your opponent, keep him/her in front of you while also being very aware of where the ball is. Your teammates are there to help as well, when the opposing team attempts to "set a pick" your teammates communicate.."pick or watch the pick" thereby allowing you to "fight" through the pick. IN YOUR WALK with God, stay focused on your tasks at hand but at the same time be aware of what is going on in the SPIRIT REALM. The Holy Ghost is a guide, he will not allow you to be "picked" off if you stay alert and listen. SEE THE BALL, SEE THE MAN!!!

Sprint To The End-Zone!!!

In football the person who carries/catches/runs with the ball needs the assistance of teammates to BLOCK the defenders. Sometimes Athletes are so talented, they can CREATE their own space... Looking at this from a spiritual perspective, God has given us the Football, the Lord of Hosts and the Angelic army has blocked the enemies of God, there are gaping holes for you to SPRINT THROUGH..Sprint until the end-zone/finish line. The enemy may come like defenders do when they CHASE the ball carrier and try to knock the ball away, but Because you HAVE FASTED, PRAYED, ENDURED,STUDIED ..your arms are too strong now for the GIFT/ MANIFESTATION, TESTIMONY too be STRIPPED AWAY....YOU HAVE CREATED SPACE BETWEEN You and the enemies..SPRINT TO THE FINISH, when you get there, no need for raucous celebration, just THANK and give God the glory and run back to your coach/ God for the next Play/ assignment.

THREE STEPS TO AVOID ACCEPTING THE AVERAGE

"AVOID ACCEPTING THE AVERAGE"

1. Use what you have, take your best assets, character traits, talents and skills and sharpen those… work at mastery of those areas.

2. Select 3 Goals to Achieve.
   a. One goal should be something that can be accomplished easily, an area where you possess mastery..why.. to have a "win."

   b. One goal should be a challenge that requires current mastery plus collaboration with others, exposure to and integration of new information/things.

   c. One goal should be-in your opinion-impossible…this will require all of the above plus faith, recognizing atmosphere shifts and the confidence to "Go For It."

3. Delight In God, Diligently Pursue "God Ordained" Plans, Devote quality time to details, Desperately Desire to Please God

—⁓⁕⁓—

An Apple for Your Thoughts

Always Available to God...A

Prayerfully Positioned To Seize Kairos Moments...P

Preparing For Increase....P

Letting Go and Leaving Behind Whatever....L

Expanding My Expectations Above and Beyond.....E

A. P. P. L. E.

The 4 A's Steps to Salvation

Acknowledge, Agree, Ask, Accept

ACKNOWLEDGE
For all have sinned, and come short of the glory of God.
(Romans 3:23 KJV)

AGREE
with John 3:16-For God so loved the world, that he gave his only begotten Son, that whosoever believeth in him should not perish, but have everlasting life. (John 3:16 KJV)

ASK
God to Forgive you from your sins (repent-turn from wrongdoing-Lord Jesus, forgive me of my sins.)

ACCEPT
Jesus Christ as your personal Savior. (Lord Jesus, I accept you today as my Lord and Savior.) That if thou shalt confess with thy mouth the Lord Jesus, and shalt believe in thine heart that God hath raised him from the dead, thou shalt be saved. For whosoever shall call upon the name of the Lord shall be saved.
(Romans 10:9, 13 KJV)

CPSIA information can be obtained
at www.ICGtesting.com
Printed in the USA
BVHW051116090122
625814BV00008B/160

9 781628 650792